LaVon Koerner

Untangling

the Seven Desires of Your Heart

God's pathway to emotional freedom

WIPF & STOCK · Eugene, Oregon

Wipf and Stock Publishers
199 W 8th Ave, Suite 3
Eugene, OR 97401

Untangling the Seven Desires of Your Heart,
The Participant's Heart Workbook
God's Pathway to Emotional Freedom
By Koerner, Lavon
Copyright©2018 SAIACS
ISBN 13: 978-1-5326-7579-9
Publication date 11/15/2018
Previously published by SAIACS, 2018

Dedicated to everyone who is experiencing suffering

(Relational, Financial, Marital, Mental, Emotional and/or Physical)

When I arrive in heaven, one of the very first things I will tell Jesus is "Thank You for the suffering you allowed me to have. I was blessed to endure it with Your gracious assistance and the measured hope You gave me daily! Without that, I would never have had the opportunity to know and trust You with me. Your loving, supportive presence and personal guidance led me through the storms of life. You were always there when I needed You. Not for a moment did You ever forsake me."

You came near when I called you,
and you said, "Do not fear."

You, Lord, took up my case;
you redeemed my life.

Lamentations 3:57-58, NIV

It took suffering to humble me and become desperate for a savior friend — Jesus! And to all of you who are experiencing hardship of any kind, this book is devoted to you. <u>Suffer well my friends, suffer well!</u> And soon, we will celebrate together in the splendor of heaven! May this book assist you in suffering well!

For I consider that the sufferings of this present time are not worthy
to be compared with the glory which shall be revealed in us.

Romans 8:18, NKJV

LaVon

Contents

Author's Introduction · 2

So Really, What's This All About? · 3

Your First Meeting With Your Group · 5

Agenda for Your First Meeting · 6

Knowing the Core Aspirations of Your Heart · 11

Are you being played by Satan? (Part A) · 16

Are you being played by Satan? (Part B) · 24

Is It Important to Be Important? · 28

Filling Each Moment With the Presence of God · 34

God Is Always Expectantly Waiting for You on the Other Side of Forgiveness · 40

God Never Intended for You to Live Life Without Him · 46

Are You Getting Enough Love? · 53

Is This a Better World Because of You? · 59

Have You Learned Contentment Yet? · 66

So Really, How Are You Feeling? · 71

Leader's Resource Guide · 77

Preparing to Lead · 78

Why the Bible Study you are leading is the very best way to develop people for Christ · 80

Note to Reader

This is a companion workbook to be utilized in a small Group study when reading
Untangling the Seven desires of Your Heart.

Invitation

As you read this book, you are cordially invited to go to the book's website to receive
additional free support resources to assist you on your journey to emotional freedom.
http://untanglingheart.com/

Author's Introduction

CRITICAL GUIDELINES FOR THE UTILIZATION OF THIS WORKBOOK

The foundational book, *Untangling the Seven Desires of Your Heart*, was designed to expose and make you mindful that buried deep in the aspirations of your own heart, there are desires that will not and must not be ignored. Each desire was purposely implanted by God in your heart to push and pull you to something bigger than yourself that resides outside of yourself. Until each of those seven desires are satisfied, they become a curse to every nonbeliever, condemning them to a life of restless pursuits, always in search of an elusive fulfillment that never comes. But to those who come to faith in God and His Son, Jesus Christ, these noisy and demanding internal desires become the doorway to a life transformation resulting in your ultimate fulfillment from the most satisfying and liberating love relationship with the most powerful person in the universe.

But that transformational process doesn't happen in a moment, in a blink of an eye; it's a journey where you personally take one desire at a time and put it on the altar and leave it in the lap of Jesus to do for you that which you cannot do for yourself. And this workbook will take you on a slow and deliberate walk forward, fully knowing that Satan will fight and deceive you every step of the way, for he knows if your journey of faith is successful, he will lose you to Jesus forever. The stakes for your future have never been higher. The eyes of eternity are upon you! And many prayers have already been made on your behalf.

Therefore, go forward with full faith, Satan be damned, looking full in the face of Jesus, listening to His beckoning call, seeing His outstretched arms ready to take you by the hand and securely lead you forward on the most liberating journey anyone can ever possibly make. Grab some buddies to travel down this road with you and take encouragement from each other. Traveling this journey alone is far too risky. Let God work through you to make others successful as others accept accountability to ensure your success. On this journey, nobody reaches the finish line all by themselves. Sadly, some will drop out, don't let that be you and for God's sake, don't let it be one of your buddies.

Remember, *Be alert and of sober mind. Your enemy the devil prowls around like a roaring lion looking for someone to devour* (1 Peter 5:8, NIV).

Sufficient is this word to the wise in this biblical warning.

LaVon

So Really, What's This All About?

ARE YOU READY FOR THIS?

Contrary to what you may be thinking, this is not about a book. It is all about, and only about you, and God's love for you, and my sincere desire that you become blown away by God's unconditional love, as am I. The biblical prayer that undergirds my writing is this: *May the Lord direct your hearts into God's love and Christ's perseverance* (2 Thessalonians 3:5, NIV). In other words, this initiative is all about allowing God to direct your heart and the seven desires He has placed there so that those desires can be met and completely fulfilled! I want you to become familiar with all seven desires and identify any existing love gaps associated with each of those desires, and then to grasp the impact those love gaps are having on your life. Thus begins our journey to emotional freedom. One by one, I want to show you how you can exchange a negative and destructive feeling emanating from an unfulfilled love gap with a positive and uplifting feeling. This can only be done by silencing the noisy clamoring and lifting the unrelenting heaviness caused by love gaps in your life. Most often, you may be oblivious to the harm they are doing to and in you. I want to alert you to the powerful influence an unfulfilled love gap can have on you. Most people are living suboptimized lives, not even knowing the massive amount of love they are leaving on the table, totally unclaimed! I want you to claim every last bit of that love and hold on to it for everything its worth, which is the absolute joy of the abundant life Jesus promised!

And even more than that, I want you to have the thrill of partnering with the only true source of all pure love in the universe and allowing His love to come gushing through you to others who are unknowingly starved for this powerful, freeing love. I want you to feel the overjoyed privilege of being picked by the God of the universe to be used as a conduit of the most healing, liberating, and satisfying love another human being could ever experience, and that you would be part of the love transformation of everyone in your Bible study group. I want you to have a front-row seat of witnessing and participating in the empowerment of other human beings as they experience an emotional jailbreak of which there is no equal. I want you to see a person's countenance being transformed from anxiousness to hopefulness and being eternally changed by having the personal involvement in the real-time fulfillment of 1 Peter 3:15. You will witness these miracles during your group's Bible study in the next 12 weeks.

… Always be prepared to give an answer to everyone who asks you to give the reason for the hope that you have … (NIV). (Emphasis mine)

Notice how the Bible suggests that witnessing conversations can often begin. They start with a nonbelieving individual encountering a mature, believing Christian and seeing an unusual and differentiating hopefulness in that person which is so highly contagious that they cannot refrain from asking questions like:

- "I noticed there is something different about you, you are so unflappable and positive, why?"
- "How can you be so optimistically confident under your circumstances? I don't know how you do it."
- "What do you know that I don't know that makes you always so cheerful?"
- "I enjoy being around you because of your enthusiasm for life, how did you get to be that way?"

A hopeful individual is a person described in *Untangling the Seven Desires of Your Heart*, a person who has traveled the journey to emotional freedom. As you share with other people as they walk down this book's journey to emotional freedom, you will have the unique blessing of being a catalyst for setting other people free from the negativity that inevitably comes from unfulfilled and unattended love gaps. God will use you to deliver people from an irrelevant life of drudgery at the worst, or from a suboptimized life at best.

Note for Bible study leader: On behalf of every person who participates in your study, thank you for being willing to show them how Christ wants to set them free from the scourge of all those negative feelings about themselves! Please read the additional instructions and information at the back of this book in the section titled "Leader's Resource Guide."

LaVon

Your First Meeting With Your Group

(Participant Workbook)

LAYING A READINESS FOUNDATION FOR LEARNING

Note for Bible study leader, pre-meeting: Before you have your first meeting, consider editing, and sending all your group participants this brief invitation (email, text, or letter).

Dear _____ ,

I'm very excited about inviting you to go on a journey to emotional freedom with me. It will take us about 12 weeks from start to finish. If you have not already done so, please obtain the book entitled *Untangling the Seven Desires of Your Heart*. Once you have your copy, please read all the front pages up to, but not including Chapter 1, and then read the Epilogue at the end of the book. This will capture not only the purpose of the book but also give you a glimpse of the potential power that the book could have on your life.

Our first meeting will be held on _____ (time to time) and take place at _____. I look forward to experiencing what God has in store for each of us as we meet and travel this journey together. I encourage you to bring a journal (a place to capture and track those breakthrough moments that we all will have on this journey).

Expectantly and lovingly,

_____ (Your Bible study leader)

Agenda for Your First Meeting

Notes for Bible study leader: View each suggested activity as optional based on your available time and participant interest.

THE TWOFOLD PURPOSE OF YOUR FIRST MEETING

Establish transparency as the standard operating norm for every meeting and build a buddy system that will foster accountability as all of you as participants embark on your journey to emotional freedom.

SET UP A WAY FOR THE GROUP TO COMMUNICATE BETWEEN MEETINGS.

This can be a group text, a Facebook account, a place for reminders, whatever works for your group. It is critical to keep this group connected electronically for the in-between times. Also, remember to establish the purpose and use of this connection, it is for X, it is not for Y, so that it remains a valuable, engaging part of this community. Set this up during the meeting.

Activity 1: Becoming a book

Note for Bible study leader: After you have opened your meeting in whatever manner you choose, remind your study colleagues of the saying, "You are the only book that some people will ever read." Given that this is true of some of the people in your personal world of contacts and connections, pause and reflect on that reality.

Each participant should ask himself or herself these questions and share their answers with the group. Use the spaces provided to jot down your answers, notes, comments, or questions.

If you were a book, what would your name (title) be?
- *In the book that we are studying, the author has put in a section cautioning the reader on the best way to read the book. (See Author's Introduction.) What would be your caution (dos and don'ts) to the people who are reading you like a book?*
- *Whom would you invite to write the foreword to your life book? What would you hope that they would say that would encourage others to read your life story?*

Use the space below to write your answers.

JOTS, THOUGHTS, AND QUESTIONS

_____
_____
_____
_____
_____
_____
_____
_____
_____
_____
_____
_____
_____
_____

Activity 2: Epilogue analysis

Note for Bible study leader: *Debrief your views of the Epilogue by asking each other these three questions:*

- *What was the writer saying in her testimony that was the most meaningful and inspiring to you?*

- *Do you think that the writer of the Epilogue is representative of you and/or people that you know? If so, how?*

- *After reading her description of her journey to emotional freedom, what excites you or scares you about taking this journey over the next 12 weeks?*

JOTS, THOUGHTS, AND QUESTIONS

1. _____
2. _____
3. _____
4. _____

Activity 3: Creating a buddy system

Note for Bible study leader: *Open the book and turn to the section of dos and don'ts in the Author's Introduction with the group. Go through all seven dos and don'ts. Discuss each one and take special note when you get to these two items:*

- *Don't read it alone, get a buddy or a small Bible study group that will hold each other accountable each step of the way. I promise you that you will have a much deeper friendship at the end of the book than you had when you began. This book will destroy superficiality and replace it with a true Christ-centered relationship. You will have some very high-impact and memorable heavenly discussions.*

- *Do ask the people reading the book with you hard questions in love as to how they are planning on applying these new breakthrough concepts into their lives. Invite them to ask you difficult questions in return. Let the verse in Proverbs 27:17 become a reality where it says, <u>As iron sharpens iron</u>, so one person <u>sharpens</u> another (NIV). (Emphasis mine) Let the sparks fly.*

If the group is large, encourage each person to get a buddy mate for the journey, making a promise to be the kind of buddy that fulfills the directive in the bullet point above. (If you have an uneven number, you can have three people in a buddy system.) They would stay buddies for the entire journey through the book.

JOTS, THOUGHTS, AND QUESTIONS

Activity 4: The most dangerous prayer in the world

When speaking, the author often shares that he had drifted away from his vibrant relationship with Christ and once he recognized it, he prayed the most dangerous prayer that a person can pray. He asked God to do whatever He needed to do to bring him back to Christ in an irrevocable personal relationship and make absolutely certain that he was ready to meet God on the judgment day. He said that God's answer was to put him through suffering which brought him back to Christ. The author cautioned us to only pray that prayer when we are really ready.

Note for Bible study leader: *Ask your group these questions.*

How do each of you feel about that prayer? Is it a dangerous prayer? Is the danger worth it? Is it more dangerous <u>not</u> to pray it?

When, if ever, would you feel comfortable saying this prayer?

JOTS, THOUGHTS, AND QUESTIONS

Activity 5: *In David's prayer in Psalm 139: 23 we are instructed to allow God to know and test our hearts.*

Search me, God, and <u>know my heart</u>; <u>test me</u> and <u>know my anxious thoughts.</u> (Emphasis mine) — Psalm 139:23, NIV

All three components of David's prayer, underlined in the verse above, are accomplished in Chapter 1 of the book. They include a) heart knowledge, b) testing, and c) the presence of anxious thoughts.

To be prepared for reading Chapter 1, become aware of the concept of a **love gap**. There are seven desires in each of our hearts and when any of these desires have not been <u>sufficiently satisfied</u>, that leaves or creates a love gap. In the first chapter, you will have the opportunity to have love gaps revealed in any of the seven desires in your hearts. But hasten to be reassured that wherever the presence of a love gap is uncovered, the rest of the book will take us on a journey to close each love gap, one at a time, resulting in the achievement of taking another step towards emotional freedom.

THIS WEEK'S TAKEAWAY

Each person should identify the single most important learning from this session, something that God is pressing on your heart to integrate into your daily lifestyle, beginning immediately this coming week.

_____

_____

_____

_____

_____

_____

_____

_____

_____

_____

_____

Note for Bible study leader: Tell the group what you hope will happen during this study and tell what you worry about most that may prevent you from having a successful study.

Assignment for next meeting: Read the first chapter, entitled "Knowing the Core Aspirations of Your Heart." This chapter will allow you to fulfill David's prayer in Psalm 139:23 where we are instructed to allow God to know our hearts!

> *Search me, God, and know my heart;*
> *test me and know my anxious thoughts.*
> (Emphasis mine) — Psalm 139:23, NIV

Note for Bible study leader: Close with prayer.

If you have selected buddies, each buddy should close by praying for their new buddy.

Chapter 1

(Participant Workbook)

Knowing the Core Aspirations of Your Heart

AGENDA FOR YOUR MEETING

Session purpose: For each individual to have a come-to-Jesus moment with their own heart

Note for Bible Study Leader

Activity 1: *Have your group discuss these two scriptural truths; make sure they are firmly in your minds at the beginning of your meeting.*

You will not know the importance of Chapter 1 until you know the truths in these two Scriptures. (These are two excellent Scriptures to memorize before the next meeting. Consider printing them on note cards.) Be creative if you want with something to put on a keychain, or post in your car, or write on your hand with a Sharpie®, or do something else.

Know this: *The heart is deceitful above all things ... (Jeremiah 17:9, NIV). (Emphasis mine)*

Do this: *Search me, God, and know my heart; test me and know my anxious thoughts (Psalm 139:23, NIV). (Emphasis mine)*

JOTS, THOUGHTS, AND QUESTIONS

_____

_____

_____

_____

Putting these two Scriptures together, back-to-back, provides the reason why the author begins the book in the way that he does.

The first Scripture informs us that we cannot always trust our own heart. It plays games with us. We are told it can hide its real feelings from us. It can hide its power over our lives, it can toy with our minds until we are confused as to what is real and what is an illusion. That is why what the world often says to us is very bad advice, sayings like "Trust your gut", or "Go with your heart." etc. Your heart is <u>no</u> substitute for prayer and the Bible and/or the counsel of a good Christian friend.

Then the second Scripture tells us how we can reveal what is really going on in our hearts. It tells us to <u>test</u> it. It tells us to uncover those deep hidden, <u>anxious thoughts</u>. It implores us to <u>know and come to terms</u> with what actually is going on in our hearts. We are told to ask God to <u>search</u> us.

By reading and applying Chapter 1's testing to your own heart, you will have implemented the second Scripture to begin detecting serious love gaps that are currently damaging your life, more than you've ever been aware of. Without this new knowledge, you cannot begin reversing the damage currently being done by the truth revealed in the first Scripture.

Note for Bible study leader

Activity 2: *You must take time to reveal your testing results following this process. (If you have a large group, you may want this to be buddy-time. Be mindful of your time limitations.)*

- *Share your scores in each area of the seven desires, and why you gave it the score you did.*

- *Share which areas have the biggest love gaps (lowest scores).*

- *Share which grouping they fall into on the scoring interpretation guide.*

- *Let each person share his/her feelings about their overall results.*

- *Share and record each other's scores.*

- *Discuss what your current greatest concern is about your results.*
- *Pray together for God to begin closing everyone's love gaps in the coming weeks.*

JOTS, THOUGHTS, AND QUESTIONS

_____

_____

_____

_____

_____

_____

_____

_____

_____

_____

_____

_____

Note for Bible study leader

Activity 3: *Buddy time if you have broken into buddies*

TAKE SOME PRIVATE TIME TO:

- Share and record each other's scores.
- Share your current greatest concern about your results.
- Pray for God to begin closing your love gaps in the coming weeks.

JOTS, THOUGHTS, AND QUESTIONS

_____

_____

_____

_____

_____

_____

_____

_____

Activity 4: A short reminder connecting this verse to any love gaps in your test results

A volunteer will read aloud this amazing Scripture: *And so, we know and rely on the love God has for us. God is love. Whoever lives in love lives in God, and God in them. (1 John 4:16, NIV). (Emphasis mine) In this book, we will refer to every area and every time where we are found not to be relying on God's love as a love gap. This will continually make it clear and remind us where we are failing to rely on and take full advantage of God's abundant love in any of the seven desires of our heart. Isn't it interesting to note that this verse does not say that we should rely on God's power or God's wisdom, but it says we should rely on God's love.*

Discuss the implications of this as a group.

JOTS, THOUGHTS, AND QUESTIONS

THIS WEEK'S TAKEAWAY

Identify the single most important learning from this session, something that God is pressing on your heart to integrate into your daily lifestyle, beginning immediately this coming week.

Assignment for next meeting: Read Chapter 2 in the book, entitled "Are You Being Played by Satan?"

This next chapter is a long one and we will be breaking it into two parts. Part A will only deal with the first of the three steps explained in the chapter, under the topic of "feeling victimized".

Note for Bible study leader: Close with prayer, but before you close make sure you all have shared how you are feeling about your heart's starting place at the beginning of this study and what your prayer is for what you are hoping to happen in the coming weeks.

Are you being played by Satan?

Suggestion: This chapter is subdivided into the following three sections showcasing how Satan attacks us.

- **Feeling victimized, Step 1**
- **Feeling abandoned by God, Step 2**
- **Not feeling afraid of Satan, Step 3**

You are encouraged to use this session to only focus on the <u>first step</u>, feeling victimized.

Session purpose: To help you to recognize when you have been duped into victim thinking and how that robs you of life's joy, power, and love. Or said another way, you must see how often and how cunningly Satan gets you to start thinking like a victim.

Note for Bible study leader

Activity 1: Understanding how Satan works

Ask a participant to volunteer to tell the story of how Satan got Adm and Eve to commit the first sin. Make sure they understand that Eve had to feel like a victim before she committed the sin. Talk about how Satan achieved that. What negative feelings did he generate in Eve's mind? How did he do that? Underscore that is the same tactic Satan uses on us today. Satan is hell-bent on getting us to think and feel like a victim. He wants you to go to bed feeling like a victim, and he wants you to wake up feeling like a victim.

JOTS, THOUGHTS, AND QUESTIONS

Activity 2: Getting in touch with what you really believe about how Satan works in and on your personal life

Chances are that many of us do not really fear Satan the way we need to. Nor do we understand the intensity with which we are being pursued by Satan.

Begin the discussion in this vital area by asking yourselves some or all of these questions:

- *Have you ever realized that you were being attacked by Satan? What was that like and how did you know it was Satan?*

- *How often do you think Satan and his demons attack you?*

- *On a scale of 1 to 10, how much do you fear Satan? Why that much?*

- *Do you believe that Satan can use your best friends to attack you?*

- *Do you believe that Satan can use your own heart to attack you?*

- *Do you believe that Satan knows the exact areas where you are most vulnerable to temptation? Can you share an area in your life where you are vulnerable?*

- *Can Satan be super nice to you? How and why would he do that?*

- *Can you be possessed by Satan in some area of your life?*

- *Can Satan tempt you into thinking everything is OK when it is not?*

- *Can Satan tempt you to become unafraid of him?*

JOTS, THOUGHTS, AND QUESTIONS

Activity 3: Getting a scriptural view of how you should think and feel about Satan

Read this Scripture and tell what it is really saying to you:

Finally, be strong in the Lord and in the strength of his might. Put on the whole armor of God, that you may be able to stand against the schemes of the devil. For we do not wrestle against flesh and blood, but against the rulers, against the authorities, against the cosmic powers over this present darkness, against the spiritual forces of evil in the heavenly places. Therefore take up the whole armor of God, that you may be able to withstand in the evil day, and having done all, to stand firm (Ephesians 6:10-13, ESV).

JOTS, THOUGHTS, AND QUESTIONS

Activity 4: *We are under Satan's constant threat to victimize us. We are warned to be vigilant regarding Satan. Mark 14:38, NKJV: Watch and pray, lest you enter into temptation. The spirit indeed is willing, but the flesh is weak.*

- *Why do you think this verse is in the Bible?*
- *What does it imply?*

Activity 5: *Those who do not yield to temptation will be rewarded. James 1:12, NKJV: Blessed is the man who endures temptation; for when he has been approved, he will receive the crown of life which the Lord has promised to those who love Him.*

How do you make the reward more appealing than the temptation?

When is the last time you really thought about heaven?

JOTS, THOUGHTS, AND QUESTIONS

Activity 6: The Victim/Victor Chart

Natural Thinking Progression	Victim Thinking (Steps Downward)	Victor Thinking (Steps Upward)
#1: Thinking's center of origin	Egocentric (Self)	Christocentric (God and others)
#2: Focused on	What I don't have	What I do have
#3: Thought pattern of	Accusing and blaming	Praying and thanking
#4: Emotional state of	Self-pity and bitterness	Appreciativeness and praise
#5: Life approach of	Deserving and entitled	Humility and gratefulness
#6: Disposition of	Doom and gloom	Hopefulness and cheerfulness
#7: Predisposed to be	Pessimistic	Optimistic
#8: Prone to feelings of	Periods of depression	Sustainable abundance of joy
#9: Yielding	Relationship conflicts	Love and forgiveness
#10: Who's in charge?	The thinking is in charge.	The thinker is in charge.

Looking at the chart, ask yourself some or all of these questions and determine what side of the chart you are on in each area:

> *Your marriage*
> *Your job/business position*
> *Your living conditions (home neighborhood, etc.)*
> *Your financial situation*
> *Your health*
> *Your car*
> *Your family's treatment of you*
> *Your vacation this year*
> *Other*

From reading this chapter, what would you have to do to get on and stay on the right side of the chart? Record your answers below.

JOTS, THOUGHTS, AND QUESTIONS

_____

_____

_____

_____

_____

_____

_____

_____

_____

_____

_____

Activity 7: Claiming a promise

Reading the 18 promises that follow, ask the Holy Spirit to direct you to the one most important promise for you individually at this particular time in your life and share it with the group. Tell why you think that God wants you to focus on that particular promise.

- **God is always available and knows your situation!** *Nahum 1:7 – The Lord is good, a stronghold in the day of trouble; he knows those who take refuge in him (ESV). (This is my loneliness buster.)*

- **He promises that you will never be tempted beyond your ability to deal with it!** *1 Corinthians 10:13 – No temptation has overtaken you that is not common to man. God is faithful, and he will not let you be tempted beyond your* *ability, but with the temptation he will also provide the way of escape, that you may be able to endure it (ESV). (I use this one a lot.)*

- **You don't ever have to be afraid!** *Proverbs 1:33 – But whoso hearkeneth unto me shall dwell safely, and shall be quiet from fear of evil (KJV). (This is my personal anxiety breaker.)*

- **God will never, ever quit on you!** *Psalms 121:8 – The LORD shall preserve thy going out and thy coming in from this time forth, and even for evermore (KJV). (This is what I use when I'm tempted to feel that God is giving up on me because I keep goofing up.)*

- **God will never ever let you down!** *Deuteronomy 31:6 – Be strong and of a good courage, fear not, nor be afraid of them: for the LORD thy God, he it is that doth go with thee; he will not fail thee, nor forsake thee (KJV). (This is my personal battle cry when I'm in the heat of a severe battle.)*

- **God will always help you when you need it!** *Psalms 46:1 – God is our refuge and strength, a very present help in trouble (KJV). (When I'm so tired and I need a place to run to find rest, this is my comfort.)*

- **God never takes His eye off you!** *Psalms 121:3 – He will not suffer thy foot to be moved: he that keepeth thee will not slumber (KJV). (This is exactly how I make sure that God is seeing what I'm seeing, and He knows what I'm dealing with.)*

- **God is bigger than your weaknesses!** *2 Corinthians 12:9 – And he said unto me, "My grace is sufficient for thee: for my strength is made perfect in weakness." Most gladly therefore will I rather glory in my infirmities, that the power of Christ may rest upon me" (KJV). (This is my go-to verse when I'm feeling weak and small.)*

- **Being poor does not disqualify you from God's help!** *Psalms 72:12-14 – For he shall deliver the needy when he crieth; the poor also, and him that hath no helper. He shall spare the poor and needy and shall save the souls of the needy. He shall redeem their soul from deceit and violence: and precious shall their blood be in his sight (KJV). (This is what I think and say to Satan when I'm feeling undeserving.)*

- **God is 100% committed to preserving you!** *Psalms 145:20 – The LORD preserveth all them that love him: but all the wicked will he destroy (KJV). (My only responsibility is to love God and love His love, and know He is taking care of all the other stuff.)*

- **He promises you that He will uphold you!** *Psalms 37:17 – For the arms of the wicked shall be broken: but the LORD upholds the righteous (NKJV). (This is my go-to verse when I feel like I'm falling or sinking.)*

- **When you doubt yourself, God wants to be your confidence!** *Proverbs 3:26 – For the LORD shall be thy confidence and shall keep thy foot from being taken (KJV). (I don't know about you, but sometimes I'm filled with doubt and am in severe need of self-confidence. This is what I speak to Satan in those times.)*

- **You don't have to worry about evil coming at you!** *2 Thessalonians 3:3 – But the Lord is faithful, who shall establish you, and keep you from evil (KJV). (I know it's wrong, but I often find myself worrying about the future; this verse is how I quiet those thoughts.)*

- **You don't have to fear death and can trust God to keep you out of hell!** *Jude 1:24 – Now unto him that is able to keep you from falling, and to present you faultless before the presence of his glory with exceeding joy (KJV). (As I was writing this, I received word that one of my high-school buddies just died. Am I next? This verse immediately dispels the worry behind those thoughts.)*

- **You can always run to God, anytime, anywhere!** *Proverbs 14:26 – In the fear of the LORD is strong confidence: and his children shall have a place of refuge (KJV). (Call me a crybaby if you want, but this is exactly how I deal with it. I run to Daddy!)*

- **You can sleep like a baby tonight!** *Proverbs 3:24 – When you lay down, you shall not be afraid: yea, you shalt lie down, and your sleep shall be sweet (KJV). (This is my favorite nighttime verse when I can't sleep at 2:00 AM.)*

- **You can rejoice in any and every situation, even right now!** *Psalms 5:11 – But let all those that put their trust in thee rejoice: let them ever shout for joy, because thou defendeth them: let them also that love thy name be joyful in thee (KJV). (When I find no joy in my current situation, I find joy in Him!)*

- **You can trust God to use others' evil intentions for good!** *Genesis 50:20a – You intended to harm me, but God intended it for good (NIV). (God never wastes anything, He will use even bad things for His good for me.)*

Note for Bible study leader: *Ask a volunteer to share a story of where something that originally seemed like bad news actually became a blessing.*

Bottom line: *If you are a Christian who has trusted your life to Christ, then nothing happens* **to** *you, but everything happens* **for** *you! (Discuss what this means.) All things work together for your good! (See Romans 8:28.) End of story! Either you believe this, or you don't. You are either a victim or a victor.*

How could or would you always be feeling if you really believed this? (Answer and discuss.)

JOTS, THOUGHTS, AND QUESTIONS

_____
_____
_____
_____
_____
_____

THIS WEEK'S TAKEAWAY

Identify the single most important learning from this session, something God is pressing on your heart to integrate into your daily lifestyle, beginning immediately this coming week. As a group or as buddies, pray for these decisions.

_____
_____
_____
_____
_____
_____
_____
_____
_____
_____

Assignment for next meeting: Your homework assignment for this week is to use that promise and write a psalm about it. It only needs to be two or three paragraphs long and needs to:

- Share both why and how this promise is important to you.
- Share how this promise makes you feel.
- Give thanks to God for the promise.

Also, study the last two steps that Satan uses in Chapter 2 and bring your personal psalm with you to the study next week.

Are you being played by Satan?

Session's double purpose: a) To know with certainty that Satan has been and is lying to you about your view of God, and b) to know that you are probably not taking Satan's hatred of you seriously enough!

> **Activity 1:** *Each person should share their homework assignment from last week where they turned a promise into a psalm. Read the psalm you wrote about the promise you selected.*
>
> *After each one of you reads your psalm, share the feelings you had both before and after you wrote the psalm claiming that promise. Help each other associate the feelings that being a victor generates in them and how they are different from those feelings of being a victim.*
>
> *Remember, this book is designed to put you on a journey to emotional freedom. Please discuss what you think that means. This will become clearer and clearer as you progress forward in the book.*

JOTS, THOUGHTS, AND QUESTIONS

_____

_____

_____

_____

_____

_____

_____

_____

Activity 2: Satan's intentional and relentless distortion of your view of God

Someone read aloud the Genesis 3 account of the first sin in human history. Notice how Satan changed Eve's view of God when he said, "For God knows that when you eat of it your eyes will be opened, and you will be like God, knowing good and evil" (Genesis 3:5, ESV).

Immediately after Satan gets Eve to feel like a victim, he gets her to question God's view of her and His love for her.

Here are the common areas where people have been played by Satan and have a distorted view or insufficient view of God. **Note for Bible study leader:** *Select and read some (one at a time) and ask if anyone has ever had these thoughts.*

- *I am not as important to God as other people are.*
- *God is much too busy being God and doesn't have time for me.*
- *Because I have messed up, God doesn't want me to have and feel good about His love.*
- *God is not going to help me until I get my act more together.*
- *If I were only as good as other people, God would bless me more because He would love me more.*
- *Had I been more talented, God would want to do more good things through me.*
- *I've screwed up and therefore have lost my opportunity to be really loved and used by God in any meaningful way.*
- *If I were only smarter and more creative, God would want to get behind me and lead me into successful initiatives that would make a big difference in people's lives.*
- *If I weren't so insignificant, I could really command more of God's attention.*
- *Can you think of others???*

JOTS, THOUGHTS, AND QUESTIONS

Activity 3: Gaining a healthy fear and respect of Satan

Once you have allowed Satan to make you a victim and have allowed Satan to distort and reduce your view of God, he can easily seduce you into taking the next step of discounting his evil intention for destroying your current life and getting you to rot in hell for all eternity.

Discuss this biblical truth until everybody gets it! It is foundational for obtaining emotional freedom. Don't continue until each of you feels you understand the horrific consequences that are at stake for you personally!

Foundational biblical truths in this chapter: *Just as in the original sin in the Bible, you have been played by Satan in this order:*

Step 1: *Satan has gotten you to see yourself as a victim, therefore*

Step 2: *Satan has now easily gotten you to question Christ's 100% love for you 100% of the time, then*

Step 3: *It is now an easy step to get you not to take Satan seriously. You have wrongfully concluded that if Christ does not take you seriously, why should Satan take you seriously? Once you have reached this conclusion, you are wide open to commit sin after sin after sin. You are now unconsciously on a slippery slope to hell and you may not even know it. Satan has planned it that way!*

You will have just been **played** *by Satan in the oldest three-step game in the world!*

Activity 4: Come to an understanding of how Satan advances his plan.

Read and discuss this Scripture. … The god of this age has blinded the minds of unbelievers, so that they cannot see the light of the gospel that displays the glory of Christ, who is the image of God (2 Corinthians 4:4, (NIV). (Emphasis mine)

After your initial discussion, ask yourselves if you have ever been blinded by Satan. If so, and we all have, share your experience and how you escaped the blindness. Allow each person in your group to talk about how you have become unblinded.

Activity 5: Buddy time

Grab your buddy and discuss and pray that this book and your study will help protect you from being blinded by Satan and turn the tables on Adam and Eve's story. Know that your eyes will be opened when you meditate on the Word of God instead of taking a bite of forbidden fruit. This book has been designed to remove the blindness to the awesomeness of Jesus!

THIS WEEK'S TAKEAWAY

Identify the single most important learning from this session, something that God is pressing on your heart to integrate into your daily lifestyle, beginning immediately this coming week.

_____

_____

_____

_____

_____

_____

_____

_____

_____

_____

Assignment for next meeting: Read Chapter 3

The next seven chapters constitute your journey to emotional freedom. As you begin addressing and managing each of the seven desires of your heart, you will begin experiencing more and more emotional freedom as each of these seven steps of your personal journey begin unfolding.

Note for Bible study leader: Each of you reshare your test score in the first of the seven desires of your hearts. Immediately close with a prayer that as each of you read the next chapter, your love gaps will start to be closed.

First desire of your heart: **Knowing and feeling you are important**

Second desire of your heart: **Knowing and feeling you are supported**

Third desire of your heart: **Knowing and feeling you are exonerated**

Fourth desire of your heart: **Knowing and feeling you are capable**

Fifth desire of your heart: **Knowing and feeling you are desirable**

Sixth desire of your heart: **Knowing and feeling you are relevant**

Seventh desire of your heart: **Knowing and feeling peaceful contentment**

Let's begin the journey to emotional freedom, one step at a time, one love gap at a time!

Chapter 3

(Participant Workbook)

Is It Important to Be Important?

Refresh your memory on the first desire God placed in your heart.

Knowing and feeling you are important: I know that I'm important because the God of the universe says I am and has demonstrated that through the death of His Son on my personal behalf. Believing and <u>relying</u> on this frees me from having to prove or spend any time trying to become important or earn importance from people or possessions, because I already have it! Because He is central to all that I do and to who I am in Christ, I have only to play to an audience of one, Jesus Christ! I'm important because He says so!

Session purpose: When you leave this meeting, we want you to know what real and authentic importance is and how you can get and keep it.

NOTES FOR BIBLE STUDY LEADER:

Opening prayer: All participants remind each other of their original love gap score in this first desire of their heart, then everyone gives a short prayer for the person on their left to get insight on how to close their love gap.

Activity 1: Divide into two subgroups.

Subgroup 1 creates a list of all the different feelings that a person who knows they are important feels.

_____

_____

_____

_____

_____

_____

Subgroup 2 creates a list of all the feelings that a person who thinks they are unimportant feels.

Do these feelings associate with one particular area of your life or just a group of people, or is it pervasive?

Compare and discuss the differences between the two lists. Each of you reveal what percentage of your time you spend in subgroup 1's listing of emotions and what percentage of your time in subgroup 2's emotions. How is that similar or dissimilar to your friends with whom you spend most of your time?

Activity 2: A get in touch introspective exercise

Each person completes this sentence: I feel important when I _____.

If you are struggling with your answers, consider these two additional questions to jump-start your thinking.

1. <u>What</u> *gives you the feeling of importance?*

2. <u>Who</u> *gives you the feeling of importance?*

JOTS, THOUGHTS, AND QUESTIONS

After everyone has pondered their answers, discuss this: Given your answers, if your sense of importance comes from these things and/or these relationships, how might you be vulnerable?

Activity 3: A discussion about a deep and provocative meaning?

What did the author mean when he said, "If you want to be important, you first have to become unimportant?" How does the Bible teach and support this? Discuss the implication of these two Scriptures on your feelings of importance.

Matthew 19:30, KJV – But many that are first shall be last; and the last shall be first.

Matthew 10:39, NIV – Whoever finds their life will lose it, and whoever loses their life for my sake will find it.

Activity 4: A Bible discussion

What did Jesus mean when He said this in Matthew 19:24? "Again I tell you, it is easier for a camel to go through the eye of a needle than for a rich person to enter the kingdom of God" (ESV).

The author talks about our self-importance being a barrier of entry. What did he mean by that?

JOTS, THOUGHTS, AND QUESTIONS

_____

_____

_____

_____

_____

_____

_____

_____

_____

How can someone become unimportant, so God can make them important? What does that look like in a person's life?

JOTS, THOUGHTS, AND QUESTIONS

_____

_____

_____

_____

_____

_____

_____

_____

_____

_____

Activity 5: Claiming real Importance

The author gives five biblical reasons to prove we are important. Which one of these five do you believe the Holy Spirit is calling to your attention right now to increase your confidence in your importance to God?

1. *My <u>exalted status</u> with God — He elevates me to a royal status (Psalm 113:7-8).*

2. *My <u>priority</u> with God because of His constant attention to me (Psalm 139:17-18).*

3. My *value* to God over all the rest of His creation (Luke 12:6-7).

4. My *worth* to God — He protects me (1 Peter 5:7).

5. My *position* in God's heart — He cares for me (Psalm 56:8).

Share which one speaks to you the loudest and explain why you think God is calling that to your attention at this time in your life.

Activity 6: A short ah-ha discussion and role-play.

Chances are that you know a person who is very prideful or a narcissist. Please have compassion on them. They are someone who has a love gap in this area of feeling important and they are trying hard to fill the discomfort of that love gap in the wrong way. They are struggling with trying to be or become important. Based on what you are learning in this chapter, you now know the only way this love gap can be filled is with Christ. No one is important unless Jesus says they are. Pray for a way to convey this message to them. Although they may not show it, they are really hurting. The feeling of unimportance is a serious and deadly feeling. Love them!

Role-play a discussion of how you assist a person who is feeling unimportant. Pretend you are on a suicide hotline.

Activity 7: The benefits of closing this love gap

Each of you finish this statement: If I know and feel important because of my relationship with God, it will free me from _____

_____

(Make sure you name all the negative feelings you previously identified in Activity 1.)

THIS WEEK'S TAKEAWAY

Identify the single most important learning from this session, something that God is pressing on your heart. What is He wanting you to learn?

JOTS, THOUGHTS, AND QUESTIONS

_____

_____

_____

_____

_____

_____

_____

_____

_____

_____

_____

Praying it forward: As a group, discuss and come up with the hardest thing(s) for you to learn about authentic importance and pray for that as you pray for the people who will be reading this chapter after you. (Remember that others have prayed for you as they studied this chapter ahead of you.)

Assignment for next meeting: Read Chapter 4.

Closing comment: There is only one book in the whole world in the whole history of mankind that identifies all the important people that have ever lived or will live. It is called the *Book of Life*. One by one, all the people eternally important to God are named in that book.

Revelation 3:5, (ESV) – *The one who conquers will be clothed thus in white garments, and I will never blot his name out of the* <u>*book of life*</u>*. I will confess his name before my Father and before his angels.* (Emphasis mine)

That is the only book that counts. If you are listed in that book, <u>that makes you important!</u> Nothing else matters — end of story!

Chapter 4
(Participant Workbook)

Filling Each Moment With the Presence of God

Refresh your memory on the second desire God placed in your heart.

Knowing and feeling you are supported: Having an ongoing, sharing, and conversational fellowship with God frees you from loneliness and from feeling left out or left behind. Any negative feelings of being ostracized or being unacceptable or being insignificant are completely countered by <u>relying</u> on your status as a child of the King, complete with all the privileges of being in the family of God. He is always there for you and is always there with you. Not for a moment will He ever forsake you.

Session purpose: For you to leave this study wanting and experiencing God's loving and supporting presence in your life, every moment of every day.

> **Activity 1:** *Share with your study colleagues your current state of feeling as you begin to read and study this chapter.*
>
> *Which of these words best describe your thoughts and/or feelings when you studied this chapter? Read the list below and then share your personal reaction when you first read this chapter. Now read the list again and identify which one best describes you. After you answer, tell how so and/or why so.*

- *I felt rescued.*

- *I felt challenged.*

- *I felt comforted.*

- *I felt exposed.*

- *I felt somewhat ashamed.*

- *I felt enlightened.*

- *I felt loved.*

- *I felt wow!*
- *I felt educated.*
- *Other*

_____

_____

_____

_____

_____

_____

_____

_____

_____

Activity 2: *Have a quick discussion of the impact of social media on the quantity and quality of relationships in this technology-connected world. Discuss why loneliness has hit an all-time high in this new technology-connected and social media age, with over 40% now claiming they have a problem with loneliness.*

What is missing in technology connections?

JOTS, THOUGHTS, AND QUESTIONS

_____

_____

_____

_____

_____

_____

_____

_____

Activity 3: Discuss emptiness versus loneliness.

The author says that many people confuse loneliness with emptiness. He says emptiness is the real problem and loneness is only a symptom. He states that if some individual fills their emptiness with the loving presence of Christ, they will not have the debilitating and severe problem of loneliness.

- *Do you agree or disagree with the author? Why or why not?*

- *What is the danger of trying to fill your emptiness with someone other than Christ?*

- *Why is it unfair for someone to be used to take the place of Christ to fill your emptiness? How is that person being placed in a no-win situation?*

JOTS, THOUGHTS, AND QUESTIONS

Remember, each desire was placed in your heart to continuously draw you back to God! Only He can fill the emptiness! Anyone else will always disappoint you.

Activity 4: A marriage discussion

The author talks about the danger of getting married to fill a personal love gap. That raises some serious questions.

1. *Do you think people (knowingly or unknowingly) selfishly get married to use another person to fill a love gap that only God can fill? If so, how can that play out? What is the danger?*

2. *Do you believe that the smaller the personal love gaps in two people, the better their marriage will be?*

3. *Have you made this mistake? If so, what should you say to your marriage partner?*

JOTS, THOUGHTS, AND QUESTIONS

Activity 5: How God fills the emptiness

When invited into your heart, Christ fills it with His loving presence and seals His continued presence with … the comfort of the Holy Spirit … (Acts 9:31, ESV). But in addition, He integrates each of us into His church with an abundance of satisfying relationships. So in Christ we, though many, form one body, and each member belongs to all the others (Romans 12:5, NIV).

The church is where broken hearts and broken lives can find a loving ministry, completing the satisfying of the emptiness. In the church, we are not alone! Discuss the healthy role of the church in your life and how you can take advantage of it and make it even more fulfilling.

How do you think God wants to use your small group in this study to fill the emptiness problem in each other's lives? Read and discuss the results on your small group implied in this Scripture. Hebrews 10:24-25, (NIV) – And let us consider how we may spur one another on toward love and good deeds, not giving up meeting together, as some are in the habit of doing, but encouraging one another—and all the more as you see the Day approaching.

Honestly, is it working in your group? How can you make it work even better?

JOTS, THOUGHTS, AND QUESTIONS

_____

_____

_____

_____

_____

_____

_____

Activity 6: Religion versus relationship

The author talks about his experience of being "14 inches away from the thrill of a lifetime!" He characterized it as moving from a religion to a relationship, from his head to his heart. He went from knowing <u>about</u> Christ to <u>knowing</u> Christ.

How would you explain the meaning of his comments about his personal transformation?

Have you had a similar experience in your life? Please share how, when, and why.

If you have not yet had a similar experience, would you like for that to happen? What must happen on your part to allow this most wonderful transformation to take place?

JOTS, THOUGHTS, AND QUESTIONS

_____

_____

_____

_____

_____

_____

_____

_____

_____

Closing comments from God:

- Hebrews 13:5b, NIV – *God has said, "Never will I leave you; never will I forsake you."*

- John 14:18, TLB – *No, I will not abandon you or leave you as orphans in the storm I will come to you.*

- Psalm 23:4, TLB – *Even when walking through the dark valley of death I will not be afraid, for you are close beside me, guarding, guiding all the way.*

How much do you really believe these three promises? How important are they to you? What difference could really believing them make on how you feel?

JOTS, THOUGHTS, AND QUESTIONS

_____

_____

_____

_____

_____

_____

_____

_____

_____

_____

_____

THIS WEEK'S TAKEAWAY

Identify the single most important learning from this session, something that God is pressing on your heart to integrate into your daily lifestyle, beginning immediately this coming week.

Praying it forward: As a group, discuss and come up with the hardest thing(s) for each participant to learn about feeling God's personal support and pray for the people who will be reading this chapter after you. (Remember that others have prayed for you as they studied this chapter ahead of you.)

Assignment for next meeting: Read Chapter 5 in your book and focus on the third desire of your heart — knowing and feeling you are exonerated.

Chapter 5

(Participant Workbook)

God Is Always Expectantly Waiting for You on the Other Side of Forgiveness

Refresh your memory on the third desire God placed in your heart.

Knowing and feeling you are exonerated: Having personally accepted the 100% forgiveness by the Supreme Judge of the universe through the total redemption of Christ on my behalf, I'm 100% free from having to prove and/or validate my goodness or worthiness to anybody. Because of His grace and mercy, I am free from having to hide any of my wrongs or missteps from anyone and am totally free to hold my head high and march straight forward in any and every situation. I **rely** not on my goodness, but on the goodness of Christ which was imputed to me at salvation.

Session purpose: Your single group purpose is to make sure that every person finishes this session feeling and celebrating being 100% forgiven, and fully capable of staying forgiven! Anything less than that is totally unacceptable.

Or, said another way, to live feeling <u>no condemnation</u> according to this verse: *There is therefore now no condemnation for those who are in Christ Jesus* (Romans 8:1, (ESV)

Activity 1: Recognizing the negative feelings that unforgiveness causes
Learn to associate your own specific negative feelings with being unforgiven. You were asked to circle the feelings you have experienced or are currently experiencing from the list below when you read this chapter. Read through them one at a time and after each one, ask, "Has anybody experienced this feeling?" Then ask, "Is anybody currently feeling any of these feelings?". If someone says yes, use this session to minister to them and set them free by receiving total forgiveness.

The top seven undesirable feelings this love gap produces are:

depression   undeserving   guilt-laden   inferior

vulnerable   disgraceful   shamed

Activity 2: Some discussion points for reaching clarity on forgiveness

- *What causes us to experience unforgiveness? Have you experienced any of these?*

  - *Conscience condemning us*
  - *Unrepented and unconfessed sin*
  - *Our created need to be holy as God is holy so we can have fellowship with Him, even while we are continuing in wrongful sin-patterns of behavior.*
  - *The Holy Spirit convicting us*

- *Is there such a thing as false guilt? Can or does Satan cause false guilt?*

  - *Can you be forgiven and still feel guilty? Explain.*

- *The author makes this statement, "To be a Christian means to forgive the inexcusable because God has forgiven the inexcusable in each of us." What does this mean?*

JOTS, THOUGHTS, AND QUESTIONS

Activity 3: *Knowing the theology of forgiveness (If anyone in your group does not currently have the assurance of their personal salvation, this would be a good time to lead them through a sinner's repentant prayer and invite Christ into their lives as their personal savior). Do that after you go through these discussion points and ask if everyone is absolutely sure they are saved.*

Answer each of the following questions with scriptural specificity: Discuss each question before you provide the Scriptures.

- *Why did our ability to get forgiven have to begin with Christ, not with us?*

  - *… While we were still sinners, Christ died for us (Romans 5:8, ESV).*

- *We love because he first loved us (1 John 4:19, ESV).*

- *Why is our ability to receive forgiveness dependent on our willingness to give forgiveness to our enemies?*

  - *For if you forgive other people when they sin against you, your heavenly Father will also forgive you. But if you do not forgive others their sins, your Father will not forgive your sins (Matthew 6:14-15, NIV).*

- *What needs to happen on our part to become eligible for receiving the gift of forgiveness?*

  - *Whoever <u>believes and is baptized</u> will be saved, but whoever does not believe will be condemned Mark 16:16, (ESV). (Emphasis mine)*

  - *… If you <u>confess with your mouth</u> that Jesus is Lord and believe in your heart that God raised him from the dead, you will be saved (Romans 10:9, ESV). (Emphasis mine)*

  - *… "<u>Repent</u> and be <u>baptized</u>, every one of you, in the name of Jesus Christ for the forgiveness of your sins. And you will receive the gift of the Holy Spirit. (Acts 2:38, NIV). (Emphasis mine)*

- *Do we, or can we, ever earn our forgiveness, or become good enough to deserve forgiveness?*

  - *For by grace you have been saved through faith. And this is not your own doing; <u>it is the gift of God</u> (Ephesians 2:8, ESV). (Emphasis mine)*

  - *Are we saved because we are good or, are we good because we are saved?*

JOTS, THOUGHTS, AND QUESTIONS

_____

_____

_____

_____

_____

_____

_____

_____

Activity 4: The consequences of giving refuge to unforgiveness in our hearts.

Not forgiving someone damages us in five different areas. Read each of them and share when you have experienced one or more of these.

Harboring unforgiveness incapacitates you to:

Make good, **objective decisions** *in many other parts of your day-by-day living and make* **healthy and fearless decisions** *for your future that are awaiting direction. (How and why is this true?)*

Have a sense of **well-being and contentment** *that all is well with your soul. (Why is this true/)*

Feel **accepted and loved by God** *in a continuous, uninterrupted, joyful relationship with Christ. (What makes this true?)*

Hear the whisper of God calling you *into new missions doing new things that advance His kingdom. (Why can't we hear God?)*

Feel completely free from your past: *no haunting skeletons in your closet, nobody coming out of the woodwork with an unforgiven indictment or charge against you and your character, etc. (What impact does this have on us?)*

Ask yourself which one of these five consequences scares and/or bothers you the most and you want to avoid it in your life.

JOTS, THOUGHTS, AND QUESTIONS

Activity 5: Satan's plan B

If Satan cannot stop you from becoming forgiven through God's grace and mercy, he resorts to making you numb to the greatness of feeling forgiven. Why would Satan do that? Of what is Satan afraid of if you feel your forgiveness?

JOTS, THOUGHTS, AND QUESTIONS

Activity 6: The divine marriage of forgiveness and forgiving

In this chapter, the author highlights the Scriptures where our personal forgiveness is tied to our willingness to also forgive others. Why do you think the Bible ties these two together?

Matthew 6:14-15, NIV – For if you forgive other people when they sin against you, your heavenly Father will also forgive you. But if you do not forgive others their sins, your Father will not forgive your sins.

Luke 6:27, NIV – "But to you who are listening I say: Love your enemies, do good to those who hate you."

Ephesians 4:32, NKJV – And be kind to one another, tenderhearted, forgiving one another, even as God in Christ forgave you.

JOTS, THOUGHTS, AND QUESTIONS

THIS WEEK'S TAKEAWAY

Identify the single most important learning from this session, something that God is pressing on your heart.

Praying it forward: As a group, discuss and come up with what was the hardest thing(s) to learn about being a forgiving and forgiven person and pray for the people who will be reading this chapter after you. (Remember that others have prayed for you as they studied this same chapter before you.)

Assignment for next meeting: Read and pray your way through Chapter 6 in your book.

In the next session, we tackle the fourth desire of our hearts: **Love gap # 4: Knowing and feeling capable versus powerless.** We all want to feel empowered!

Chapter 6

(Participant Workbook)

God Never Intended for You to Live Life Without Him

Refresh your memory on the fourth desire God placed in your heart.

Knowing and feeling capable: Because I have complete faith in His promise that He will never, ever allow me to be put into a situation from which He is unable to deliver me, I'm free from having to worry or have any anxiety about what may or may not befall me. By faith, I *rely* on his available grace to confront and be victorious over any and every obstacle. His help and strength are always just a prayer away.

Session purpose: Declaring war on helplessness. No one should leave this meeting feeling helpless!

> **Activity 1:** *Read the list of the top seven negative feelings generated by a love gap in this area, where a person does not feel capable in every situation which can or is confronting them.*
>
> *The top seven undesirable feelings this love gap produces are:*
>
> | | | |
> |---|---|---|
> | inadequateness | uneasiness | future |
> | intimidated | nervous | anxiety |
> | fearfulness | overwhelmed | edginess |
>
> *Reread the list of unpleasant feelings above and identify those that you have had or are currently experiencing. (Reveal how you feel right now about various things in your lives. You can consider questions like, "What percentage of my time would you say that you feel that way?" "Are you more susceptible and vulnerable to one or two of these feelings over the others?"*

JOTS, THOUGHTS, AND QUESTIONS

_____

_____

_____

_____

_____

_____

_____

_____

_____

_____

_____

Only after you feel you've had a really good and transparent discussion, move on to the next activity.

Activity 2: *Read this verse in Timothy 1:7 (KJV). For God hath not given us the spirit of <u>fear</u>; but of <u>power</u>, and of <u>love</u>, and of a <u>sound mind</u>. (Emphasis mine) (You may want to compare different translations.)*

Discuss the differences between these words and the feelings you just previously discussed.

- *Power*
- *Love*
- *Sound mind*

Now address these two questions:

1. *Can you have both this set of feelings (power, love, sound mind) and the seven negative feelings listed at the same time? Why or why not?*

2. *The author says that you can't just pray these individual feelings into your life. They can only be present in your life when God (Christ, Holy Spirit) is the complete Lord of your life and you are surrendered to Him. He says you can't just have these pieces of God, you must seek to have all of God or none of Him. What does he mean by all of that? Do you agree? Do you think people understand this?*

JOTS, THOUGHTS, AND QUESTIONS

Activity 3: Understanding the root cause of Superstition:
Please share the strangest "Superstition" Stories you've seen or experienced.

Write and then discuss your answers to these three questions:

1. *If a person has a superstition, what does that have to do with this love gap?*

2. *Why are Ouija® boards (also known as spirit boards or talking boards) on the rise? What does that say about our society today?*

3. *What about the growing occult movement? (The supernatural, the paranormal, supernaturalism, magic, black magic, witchcraft, sorcery, necromancy, wizardry,*

the black arts, occultism, diabolism, devil worship, devilry, voodoo, hoodoo, white magic, witchery, mysticism) How does all of this relate to this love gap?

(Record your responses and thoughts in the spaces provided below and on the next page.)

JOTS, THOUGHTS, AND QUESTIONS

Each of you in your group to determine your current understanding of the harm of being superstitious by addressing these questions.

Read and answer each question as being true or false.

1. Being a little superstitious is no big deal. _____

2. Having a lucky charm does not interfere with, nor compete with, my relationship with God. _____

3. Some superstition is good, it keeps me alert and on my toes. _____

4. There is no relationship between being a little superstitious and Satan worship. _____

5. Simple acts like knocking on wood or crossing your fingers <u>are not</u> substitutes for prayer. _____

6. Avoiding the number 13 does not open the door for Satan. _____

7. Superstitions and Satan worship only happen in third-world countries. _____

8. The less academically educated you are, the more likely you are to be superstitious. _____

9. There is no relationship between being a little superstitious and opening the door to Satan in your life. _____

10. God doesn't really care if you are a little superstitious. _____

Answers: The answer to all 10 questions above is false. Discuss your differences

Use these Scriptures to underscore the danger of superstitions if needed.

The commandments forbid the worship of idols and images. Exodus 20:3-6, NIV – *"You shall have no other gods before me. You shall not make for yourself an image in the form of anything in heaven above or on the earth beneath or in the waters below. You shall not bow down to them or worship them; for I, the LORD your God, am a jealous God, punishing the children for the sin of the fathers to the third and fourth generation of those who hate me, but showing love to thousands who love me and keep my commandments."* (Emphasis mine)

Being superstitious is a form of idolatry. Idolatry worships the created rather than the Creator. Romans 1:22-23, TLB – *Claiming themselves to be wise without God, they became utter fools instead. And then, instead of worshiping the glorious, ever-living God, they took wood and stone and made idols for themselves, carving them to look like mere birds and animals and snakes and puny men.*

Activity 4: The distance between you and answered prayer

The author draws a comparison between being able to see answered prayer and sitting in the cheap seats at a sports game, so far up that you can't see the action down on the field with any clarity. What is the point he was making with this comparison?

JOTS, THOUGHTS, AND QUESTIONS

Consider your answers to these questions to assist in calibrating how much you are in the game.

- How many <u>specific</u> (not general stuff) answered prayers can you attest to in the last seven days?

- What does this say about the quality of your prayer life?
- What would be a good answer for a healthy prayer life?
- Are your prayers and their answers about you or others?
  - If they are more about you than others, what does that mean?
  - If they are more about others than your own self-interests, what does that mean?
- Given the answers above, what is your conclusion about the current status of your prayer life?
  - How could you get more into the game?
  - Should everybody be in the game?
  - Name some in the game ideas in which you could be involved. (Think of the "games" or "ministries" in which you could become involved or new ministries that you could start.

Caution, this exercise is not intended to produce false guilt or to induce guilt motivated activity in you. It is intended to cause a serious reflection on your current status of experiencing a successful and productive prayer life. It is to increase your desire to have a more powerful prayer life that will benefit both you and others that you love.

JOTS, THOUGHTS, AND QUESTIONS

THIS WEEK'S TAKEAWAY

Identify and share the single most important learning from this session, something that God is pressing on your heart.

_____
_____
_____
_____
_____
_____
_____
_____
_____
_____

Praying it forward: As a group, discuss and come up with what was the hardest thing(s) for each participant to learn about being and feeling capable and pray for the people who will be reading this chapter after you. (Remember that others have prayed for you as they studied this chapter before you.)

Assignment for next meeting: In the next session we tackle the fifth desire in our heart: **Love gap #5: Knowing and feeling you are desirable versus undesirable:** We all want to feel desired and loved. Read and pray your way through Chapter 7 in your book before next week's meeting.

Chapter 7

(Participant's Workbook)

Are You Getting Enough Love?

Refresh your memory on the fifth desire God placed in your heart.

Knowing and feeling you are desirable: Because I know that God has His undivided attention on me every minute of every day, and He is personally blessed by my love for Him and my dependence on Him and my eagerness to be totally with Him in all that I do, I'm free not to have to be seen or told or have to prove that I'm desirable or acceptable by anyone else. I'm always wanted by the only one that ultimately matters — God. It is on His promise to love me unconditionally, that I *rely*. He wants and desires to spend time with me. He is blessed by my praise, and He is jealous when I ignore Him for other things of far less value and worth. He wants all of me all the time every minute of every day. I am His, and He is mine!

Session purpose: Knowing and receiving God's total love in abundance and feeling loved every minute of every day, despite all current circumstances!

Activity 1: *Which of these feelings have you experienced or are you currently experiencing? The top seven undesirable feelings this love gap produces are:*

depression   undeserving   guilt-laden   inferior

vulnerable   disgraceful   shamed

Please share which feelings you have or are experiencing. After reading this chapter, do you have a new idea as to what could be the root cause of your feelings?

JOTS, THOUGHTS, AND QUESTIONS

_____

_____

_____

_____

_____

_____

Activity 2: If God really loves me, why does He let bad things happen to me?

*The author makes this bold comment, "God allows bad things to happen to you **to** accomplish good things that He wants to happen **for** you."*

What does the author mean by this? Do you believe this? Can you reflect on a time when something bad happened to you but looking back on it, you can now see that God used it for your good? (See Romans 8:28)

JOTS, THOUGHTS, AND QUESTIONS

_____

_____

_____

_____

_____

_____

_____

_____

_____

As a Christian, you can be certain that there is a **purpose** behind every **problem**!

If you believe that, then your desirability on God's part is not diminished just because you are experiencing difficulties. True?

- Do you really believe this?
- If you did, how would believing this impact your feelings? Why?
- If you need to increase your faith in this area, what will you need to do? (Hint: Romans 10:17)

JOTS, THOUGHTS, AND QUESTIONS

Activity 3: Confronting and confessing our personal fears

The author tells his story of overcoming his stage-fright. He says his shyness and fear of speaking were signs of his sin of being too self-absorbed and self-centered. He was not able to overcome them until he confronted and confessed them as sin.

This raises a number of very personal questions: (Discuss each question in your group.)

- *Do you believe the author is correct in calling these sins? (Shyness, stage fright, fear of speaking???)*

- *Of what are they a sign of in your own life?*

- *Can we be sinful by being over-concerned as to what people think of us?*

- *If so, with what negative results might we be bringing onto ourselves?*

- *Can our people-pleasing tendencies be sinful (pros and cons)?*

After having this discussion, what conclusions are you reaching for yourself concerning some of the inhibiting feelings that we far too often allow to hold us back?

JOTS, THOUGHTS, AND QUESTIONS

Activity 4: Our hiding places

In the book, the passage from Genesis 3 is quoted to show how Adam and Eve responded to their sin with negative feelings of fear and thereby went into hiding. The author talks about their use of fig leaves to hide. Today, we use more sophisticated hiding places to cover-up our imperfections and to make ourselves look good. The author stated examples like:

> *Homes*

> *Titles*

> *Cars*

Please finish the list through a discussion of popular hiding places in today's culture:

-
-
-
-
-

When we hide we are covering up something. What is it we are covering up?

How can we stop the urge to hide? What must we do?

JOTS, THOUGHTS, AND QUESTIONS

Activity 5: How full is your love tank?

On a scale of 1 to 100, where would you say you currently are? (Draw the dial in your gauge.)

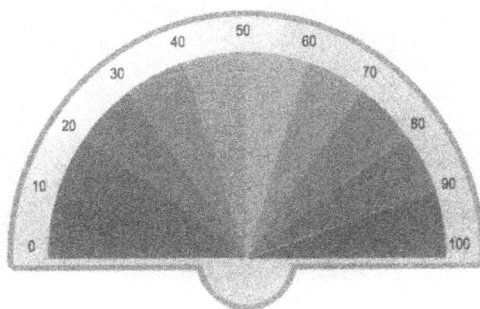

THIS WEEK'S TAKEAWAY

Some promises to overcome fear, intimidation, and being too self-absorbed.

Select only one of the following promises to dwell on this coming week. Which one did you pick? Why?

- How can we handle our fears? By believing God's promise. Isaiah 41:10, NKJV – *"Fear not, for I am with you; Be not dismayed, for I am your God. <u>I will strengthen you, yes, I will help you, I will uphold you with My righteous right hand."</u>* (Emphasis mine)

- When fearful, remember God. Joshua 1:9, NKJV – *" Have I not commanded you? Be strong and of good courage; <u>do not be afraid, nor be dismayed, for the LORD your God is with you wherever you go."</u>* (Emphasis mine)

- We simply need to love more. 1 John 4:16-18, ESV – *"So, we have come to know and to believe the love that God has for us. God is love, and whoever abides in love abides in God, and God abides in him. By this is love perfected with us, so that we may have confidence for the day of judgment, because as he is so also are we in this world. There is no fear in love, <u>but perfect love casts out fear. For fear has to do with punishment, and whoever fears has not been perfected in love.</u>* (Emphasis mine)

- Do not be afraid of people. Hebrews 13:6, TLB – *That is why we can say without any* *doubt or fear, "The Lord is my Helper and <u>I am not afraid of anything that mere man can do to me.</u>"* (Emphasis mine)

Praying it forward: As a group, discuss and come up with a list of what was the hardest thing(s) for each one of you to learn about **knowing and feeling you are desirable versus undesirable** and pray for that as you pray for the people who will be reading this chapter after you. (Remember that others have prayed for you as they studied this same chapter.)

Assignment for next meeting: In the next session we tackle the fifth desire in our heart, **love gap #6: Knowing and feeling you are relevant versus irrelevant.** We all want to feel relevant. Read and pray your way through Chapter 8 in your book.

Chapter 8
(Participant Workbook)

Is This a Better World Because of You?

Read and refresh your memory on the sixth personal heart desire that God has placed in your heart.

Knowing and feeling you are relevant: Because I've been personally designed by God and have been placed on planet earth by Him at this particular time in this particular place, I'm totally free to both know and feel empowered to enthusiastically charge straight into living every day to His glory. By faith, I know that He has designed me with purpose. Believing this, allows me to *rely* on His sovereign plan for my life. He will not waste or let go unused any situation that comes my way, whether it be good or evil. He will use it for His intended purpose, making me relevant to His will for the people He has providentially brought into my life. He is counting on me and more than anyone else, He believes in me!

Session purpose: To increase your personal sense of relevance through intensifying your connectedness to transcendent thinking — heavenly mindedness

> **Activity 1:** *Review of the eighth chapter in the book on becoming relevant*
>
> *Here is a partial list of feelings to which we are susceptible if we do not have a strong sense of relevance. Circle the ones around which you have sensitivities.*
>
> *inconsequential   insignificant   unimportant   meaningless*
>
> *inapt   purposeless   unsuitable   Insecure   despair*

> **Activity 2:** *The author talked about being in God's will or on plan. Which of these biblical principles resonate or hit home with you?*
>
> - *God has a special purpose for each of us.*
> - *God wants you to know that you are on plan.*
> - *The chapter identified a five-step approach to getting on plan. After reading this,*

which of these best represents where you are:

- ○ *I'm currently on plan.*
- ○ *No, but I want to be on plan.*
- ○ *I now feel confident that I can get to be on plan.*

JOTS, THOUGHTS, AND QUESTIONS

The author identifies two common mistakes we are prone to make when being in the center of God's will for our lives. Do either of these describe you?

- Tied up at the dock.
- Stuck on the top step.

JOTS, THOUGHTS, AND QUESTIONS

- The author shares two revealing questions that can indicate whether or not you are on plan. How did you answer these?
  - ◦ If you were to die right now, who in your life would miss your spiritual input and influence — big-time?
  - ◦ If you were to die right now, who would begin immediately missing the critical prayer benefits that come from your continued and consistent praying for that individual?

JOTS, THOUGHTS, AND QUESTIONS

_____

_____

_____

_____

_____

_____

_____

_____

_____

_____

Activity 3: *(This is new material, not included in the book. It is featured here for those of you who want to super-charge your feelings of relevance by connecting what you are currently doing and thinking with its eternal impact.) The ultimate and highest degree of relevance is being heaven bound and knowing and feeling it. Following is a test for assessing your current personal amount of heavenly mindedness.*

Answer each of the following questions by circling the answer that best represents your spiritual thinking habits regarding heaven.

1. *I think of and about heaven.*
    a. *Every day*
    b. *Regularly but not daily*
    c. *Occasionally when the subject comes up*
    d. *Seldom*

2. *I have a keen interest in heaven and study the Scriptures and what they say about it.*
    a. *It is one of my top areas of focus and contemplation.*

      b. When the issue arises, I will pursue it and study to get answers.

      c. I typically wait for others to bring the subject of heaven up, then I will pursue it and engage in a serious study of it to get clarity in some area concerning it.

      d. Heaven is just not a common or regular subject in which I have been interested in researching on any regular basis.

3.   *In the last 12 months, I intentionally discussed heaven with others.*

      a. Often, it is one of my favorite discussion points.

      b. I will proactively bring it up with the people I'm with when I feel comfortable.

      c. Really, I usually only find myself discussing it after someone or something puts the subject on the table.

      d. It is seldom a serious topic of discussion with the people with whom I interface.

4.   *I meditate and pray about heaven.*

      a. I'm always discussing heaven with God and constantly thanking Him for that promise and find myself daydreaming about it regularly.

      b. I bring it up only when I'm under emotional stress or in physical pain and begin thinking of heaven as the ultimate escape.

      c. I find myself discussing heaven with God reactively when I'm in the presence of death, terminal illness, and funerals.

      d. Although I know heaven is in my future, I don't talk to God much about heaven in my prayer life.

5.   *I connect what I'm doing to its heavenly impact.*

      a. I'm constantly thinking about the heavenly consequences of what I'm doing at the time and how it matters from an eternal perspective.

      b. I do what I do and then often review my week's actions in light of their heavenly consequences on a Sunday, or at some later time, and sometimes I am disappointed in what I did or didn't do, or my motives for doing it.

      c. I will only weigh the impact of my actions on eternity when I am in a situation. where there must be something or someone that triggers it and I'm emotionally forced to think about it.

      d. Even though I believe in heaven, I pretty much live my life without too much thought about the connectedness between what I'm doing daily and its eternal consequences.

Scoring: Award the following points:

    a) = 20 points
    b) = 15 points
    c) = 10 points
    d) = 5 points

Your total points: _____

YOUR HEAVENLY MINDEDNESS INDEX™ INTERPRETATION:

85 – 100 points = **Heavenly minded** (It constantly provides you living perspective and a strong sense of relevance. You are immune to the craziness that affects those who are not anchored in eternity.)

65 – 80 points = **Heavenly aware** (It is there when you need it in an emotional crisis, but you have to abruptly be stopped to put things into eternal perspective. Then you can regain your perspective.)

45 – 60 points = **Heaven deafness** (You are forfeiting heaven's power for continued joy in all circumstances and are detached from that wonderful sense of relevance that makes life so valuable and compelling.)

25 – 40 points = **Earth captive** (You are being imprisoned by too much earth noise, and because of that you are becoming disconnected to God's will for your life and are very vulnerable to hopelessness, and life fatigue.)

Understand the implications and identify the emotional vulnerabilities of not having a high **Heavenly Mindedness Index™** score above.

Which of the following emotional states are you susceptible to experiencing?

Despair	Discouragement
Discontent	Self-pity
Impatient	Future fearfulness
Feeling unfairly treated	Depression and/or despair
A general sad countenance	Feeling of out of control
Low enthusiasm/energy levels	Limited and/or low confidence
Fear of death	Easily shaken
Feelings of hopelessness	Too quick to judge (judgmental)
Feeling of distance between you and God	Feeling of being ungrounded
Low courage level	Susceptible to intimidation

Activity 4: *If you are concerned about what the above exercise revealed and what emotional vulnerability risks your life may have because of your current Heavenly Minded Index™, read and ponder the significance of these six verses (pictures of heaven). They are six different scriptural snapshots of heaven. God, in His wisdom and love, wants all of us to be enchanted by heaven, so the Bible gives us these six different views as to what heaven is like. We all go through different seasons in our life, so depending on where you are right now as you read this, most likely one of these will ring true in your heart more so than the others. Circle the one that has the greatest emotional appeal to you and share with your Bible study partners as to why you feel so drawn to this particular promised view of heaven at this current time in your life.*

1. *For those of us who have not experienced the guarded and continued comforts of home,* **heaven is a place that will be home to us:** *John 14:2-3a, TLB. "There are many homes up there where my Father lives, and I am going to prepare them for your coming. When everything is ready, then I will come and get you, so that you can always be with me where I am."*

2. *Many of us have yearned of taking a dream vacation to see things that others see, but we cannot.* **This view of heaven says we will have an unequaled and thrilling adventure:** *1 Corinthians 2:9, NLT. ... "No eye has seen, no ear has heard, and no mind has imagined what God has prepared for those who love Him."*

3. *Let this sink in; it is how Isaiah described heaven. It is for those of us who are bothered about all the injustices and inequalities of this life.* **Heaven is a place where there is no injustice:** *Isaiah 65:21-23, NIV. They will build houses and dwell in them; they will plant vineyards and eat their fruit. No longer will they build houses and others live in them, or plant and others eat. For as the days of a tree, so will be the days of my people; my chosen ones will long enjoy the works of their hands. They will not labor in vain, nor will they bear children doomed to misfortune; for they will be a people blessed by the LORD, they and their descendants with them.*

4. *For those of us who are so tired of violence,* **peace will pervade even the animal kingdom**: *Isaiah 65:25, NIV. "The wolf and the lamb will feed together, and the lion will eat straw like the ox, but dust will be the serpent's food. They will neither harm nor destroy in all my holy mountain, says the LORD."*

5. *For those of us who have had to contend with our feebleness and physical limitations,* **heaven will a place where the weak and handicapped will be healed and made strong:** *Isaiah 35:5-6a, NIV. Then will the eyes of the blind be opened and the ears of the deaf unstopped. Then will the lame leap like a deer, and the tongue of the dumb shout for joy.*

6. *For those of us who have experienced hardships and suffering,* **heaven will be a place where God will live with His people and there will be an end to loneliness, death, crying, and pain:** *Revelation 21:3-4, NIV. And I heard a loud voice from the throne saying, "Look! God's dwelling place is now among the people, and he will dwell with them. They will be his people, and God himself will be with them and be their God. He will wipe every tear from their eyes. There will be no more death or mourning or crying or pain, for the old order of things has passed away."*

<u>Believe in</u> and <u>live for</u> heaven. There is no better place and no better way! Our hearts long for it because it fulfills our heart's desire to be relevant!

THIS WEEK'S TAKEAWAY

Identify the single most important learning from this session, something that God is pressing on your heart to integrate into your daily lifestyle, beginning immediately this coming week.

_____

_____

_____

_____

_____

_____

_____

_____

_____

_____

Assignment for next meeting: In the next session we tackle the seventh desire in your heart, **Love gap #7: Feeling and knowing contentment versus discontent.** We all hunger for contentment. Read and pray your way through Chapter 9 in your book.

Note for Bible Study Leader

Praying it forward: As a group, discuss and come up with the hardest thing(s) for each of you to learn and apply about **knowing and feeling you are relevant versus irrelevant.** Make a list and then pray specifically for those personal insights and challenges for the people who will be reading this chapter following you. (Remember that other people, who have gone before you, have prayed for you when they studied this same chapter and made their list of difficult challenges. They prayed that <u>you</u> can overcome the challenges you have identified. Now it's your turn, out of love, to pray it forward.)

Chapter 9

(Participant Workbook)

Have You Learned Contentment Yet?

Read and refresh your memory on the seventh personal heart desire that God has placed in your heart.

Knowing and feeling a peaceful contentment. Because I've found sufficient joy and satisfaction in Him, and because I totally believe and rely on God, who promised me that He would supply all that I need, that enables me to experience a serene and tranquil contentment. My days are filled with thanksgiving. As the psalmist says, *The LORD is my shepherd, I shall not want* (Psalm 23:1, KJV). I wake up in the morning feeling very blessed and fulfilled and therefore am not susceptible to the constant prodding and pressure to continually want more. I have no desire to sacrifice my peacefulness by jumping on a treadmill that is leading nowhere and that would make me overly busy pursuing more possessions, chasing more things that will not give me the satisfaction that I'm already experiencing in my daily walk with Christ. I treasure and protect my calm and peaceful contentment. Do I know and feel peaceful contentment amongst tragic circumstances in my life?

Session purpose: To experience and sustain peace that passes all understanding

A warning! This chapter was not written to make you discontent with your contentment. That would be counterproductive. Knowing this, to some degree you will always have a certain amount of discontent in your life because you are not yet in heaven, and you are not yet 100% sanctified. But you can have areas in your life and times in your life when you are experiencing a wonderful emotional serenity that simply is not available to those outside of Christ. It is to this end that this chapter was written. Just like Paul, you have the privileged opportunity to learn contentment as you move forward in your love relationship with Christ.

Activity 1: Recognizing the emotional damage of being or remaining discontent

To find out if God wants you to focus on learning contentment, simply circle any of these common feelings of discontent that you may have had or, are currently experiencing.

displeased,   cheated,   wronged,   ill-at-ease,   restless,   bitterness,   unhappiness,   ungratified,   dissatisfied,   disgruntled,   and anxiousness

If you have circled any of these emotions, answer these questions in the space below and share with your group:

- *Is this feeling a general, overall feeling or is this feeling pretty much coming from just one or more areas in your life?*

- *After reading this chapter, do you have an idea from what it is being generated?*

- *Is it something that you and your group can and should pray for removal?*

JOTS, THOUGHTS, AND QUESTIONS

_____

_____

_____

_____

_____

_____

_____

_____

_____

_____

Activity 2: Are you winning the counterculture war?

The author states that the consumer culture in which we live is at war with the simple lifestyle of a Christian. Greed and contentment cannot reside in the same heart. Neither can covetousness and contentment. So, the question that each of us must answer is, how am I doing in the counterculture war? More specifically, how would you answer each of these questions?

Do you compare your home to those of others?

Do you compare your car with those of others?

Do you compare your wardrobe with those of others?

Do you compare your vacations with those of others?

Do you, etc.?

JOTS, THOUGHTS, AND QUESTIONS

_____

_____

_____

_____

_____

_____

_____

_____

_____

_____

If any of these questions were answered with a yes by you, then how can you become countercultural to the consumerism that is so prevalent in our society? (Discuss as a group.)

Which of these Scriptures touch your heart and could help you win the war?

- Luke 3:14, KJV – *And the soldiers likewise demanded of him, saying, "And what shall we do?" And he said unto them, "Do violence to no man, neither accuse any falsely; and be content with your wages."* (Emphasis mine)

- Hebrews 13:5, KJV – *Let your conversation be without covetousness; and be content with such things as ye have: for he hath said, I will never leave thee, nor forsake thee.* (Emphasis mine) Things don't and cannot satisfy, only Jesus can!

- Psalms 37:16, KJV – *A little that a righteous man hath is better than the riches of many wicked.* (Emphasis mine)

- 1 Timothy 6:8, KJV – *And having food and raiment let us be therewith content.* Everything else is an added blessing.

- Ecclesiastes 5:10, KJV – *He that loveth silver shall not be satisfied with silver; nor he that loveth abundance with increase: this is also vanity.* Most of us have fallen for Satan's lies that wealth will make us happy.

- 1 Corinthians 7:20, KJV – *Let every man abide in the same calling wherein he was called.* Stop coveting other people's jobs and their titles and stop comparing yourself to other people.

- Matthew 11:28, NIV – *"Come to me, all you who are weary and burdened, and I will give you rest."* (Emphasis mine) Rest equals contentment.

- Proverbs 3:5-6, NIV – *Trust in the LORD with all your heart* and lean not on your own *understanding; in all your ways submit to him, and he will make your paths straight.* (Emphasis mine) Discontent is the result of distrust.

Activity 3: Clearing your conscience

The Bible makes it clear that it is impossible to have contentment with a guilty conscience. If there is any part of your life that is not aligned with Christ, removing that is job number one. As a group, please hit the pause button and allow time for personal introspection and if necessary, confession and prayers of forgiveness.

Activity 4: *The book lays out and explains a seven-step Contentment Learning Process. Here are their headings. Please score how you are doing in each step (1=low and 5=high). Reference them in your book if necessary.*

_____ 1. *Guard your heart.*

_____ 2. *Become grateful.*

_____ 3. *Take control of your thoughts.*

_____ 4. *Break the habit of satisfying discontent with acquisitions.*

_____ 5. *Stop comparing yourself to others.*

_____ 6. *Help others.*

_____ 7. *Be content with what you have, but never be content with the progress you are making.*

_____ 8. *Pray it and leave it! If you aren't praying, you will never be content.*

Share your scores with your colleagues and let the one with the strongest score in each area share what he/she is doing to get that score.

THIS WEEK'S TAKEAWAY

Identify and share the single most important learning from this session, something that God is pressing on your heart.

_____

_____

_____

_____

_____

_____

_____

_____

_____

_____

_____

Assignment for next meeting: In the next session we conclude the journey to emotional freedom. Read Chapter 10 in your book, entitled "So Really, How Are You Feeling?"

Note for Bible Study Leader

Praying it forward: As a group, discuss and come up with the hardest thing(s) for each of you as you learn and apply about these lessons about **knowing and feeling contentment versus discontent.** Make a list by everybody contributing and then pray specifically for those personal challenges as you pray for the people who will be reading this chapter after you. (Remember that other people, who have gone before you, have prayed for you when they studied this same chapter and made their list of difficult challenges. They prayed that you can overcome the challenges they have identified. Now it's your turn, out of love, to pray it forward.)

Chapter 10
(Participant Workbook)

So Really, How Are You Feeling?

Summary of all seven love gaps: Celebrating God's provision of emotions.

Session purpose: To bring all the concepts together and learn how to get and sustain emotional freedom.

Activity 1: Made in His image

Discuss as a group: The author paints a scriptural description of an emotional God. How do you react to that characterization of God? By attaching the word "emotional" in front of God, does that weaken or strengthen your view of God? How does understanding that our God is emotional differentiate Christianity from the gods of false religions? Do you like God being emotional? Why?

JOTS, THOUGHTS, AND QUESTIONS

_____

_____

_____

_____

_____

_____

_____

_____

_____

_____

off

off

off

off

off

off

off

off

off

off

off

Activity 2: Understanding God's design and purpose for emotions

The author makes this statement about emotions, "Our emotions are misused, abused, and underused. I'm convinced that our emotions are the most underleveraged part of God's creation."

What does he mean by this?

What are the purposes of emotions? Why did God create us with the capacity to feel? (Discuss and make a list)

JOTS, THOUGHTS, AND QUESTIONS

Activity 3: Guiding emotions
When discussing emotions, the author uses the phrase Life Navigation System. What does this imply?

JOTS, THOUGHTS, AND QUESTIONS

_____

_____

_____

_____

_____

Activity 4: Exchanging negative emotions for positive ones

EMOTIONAL FREEDOM EXCHANGE

(How and why to exchange your negative emotions for positive emotions)

So, are you prepared to respond quickly and accurately when you have negative or defeating feelings? Or will they catch you off guard, creating an opening for Satan to exploit? Let's test your readiness and then improve it!

Instructions: This exercise is designed to help you familiarize yourself with knowing how to pray, what to pray for, when to pray, and what to do when you are feeling restrained by any of these common negative and defeating feelings. Draw a line from the negative emotions on the left to the proper love gap in the middle and onto the freeing positive emotions on the right. Once you've completed your answers and checked your answers against those on the Emotional Freedom Exchange answer page on the following page, you can then read the appropriate love gap chapter to know how you can facilitate the Emotional Freedom Exchange in your heart. *Then you will know the truth, and the truth will set you free. So if the Son sets you free, you will be free indeed* (John 8:32, 36 NIV).

Turn the page and see how well you do in recognizing the real source of any negative feelings that you may be experiencing.)

Restraining & Defeating Negative Emotions	Love-Gaps (Chapter Location)	Freeing & Inspiring Positive Emotions
Trivial, Inconsequential, Insignificant, and Passed-Over	Knowing and Feeling Supported Versus Alone (Chapter 4)	Wanted, Sought-After, Needed, and Looked For
Unimportant, Meaningless, Inapt, and Unsuitable	Knowing and Feeling Important Versus Unimportant (Chapter 3)	Essential, Vital, Critical, and Necessary
Condemned, Ashamed, Unworthy, and Embarrassed	Knowing and Feeling Contentment Versus Discontent (Chapter 9)	Reinforced, Empowered, Accompanied, and Escorted
Inadequateness, Weakness, Intimidated, and Nervous Anxiety	Knowing And Feeling Relevant Versus Irrelevant (Chapter 8)	Cheerfulness, Serenity, Peaceful Satisfaction, and Ease Of Mind
Unwanted, Rejected, Repugnant, and Unlovable	Knowing and Feeling Exonerated Versus Guilty (Chapter 5)	Significant, Crucial, Indispensable, and Wanted
Forsaken, Abandoned, Alone, and Forgotten	Knowing and Feeling Desirable Versus Undesirable (Chapter 7)	Confident, Prepared, Courageous, and Fearless
Restlessness, Unsettled, Ill-at-ease, and Anxiousness	Knowing and Feeling Capable Versus Powerless (Chapter 6)	Purified, Forgiven, Cleansed, and Acquitted

Restraining & Defeating Negative Emotions	Love-Gaps (Chapter Location)	Freeing & Inspiring Positive Emotions
Trivial, Inconsequential, Insignificant, and Passed-Over	Knowing and Feeling Supported Versus Alone (Chapter 4)	Wanted, Sought-After, Needed, and Looked For
Unimportant, Meaningless, Inapt, and Unsuitable	Knowing and Feeling Important Versus Unimportant (Chapter 3)	Essential, Vital, Critical, and Necessary
Condemned, Ashamed, Unworthy, and Embarrassed	Knowing and Feeling Contentment Versus Discontent (Chapter 9)	Reinforced, Empowered, Accompanied, and Escorted
Inadequateness, Weakness, Intimidated, and Nervous Anxiety	Knowing And Feeling Relevant Versus Irrelevant (Chapter 8)	Cheerfulness, Serenity, Peaceful Satisfaction, and Ease Of Mind
Unwanted, Rejected, Repugnant, and Unlovable	Knowing and Feeling Exonerated Versus Guilty (Chapter 5)	Significant, Crucial, Indispensable, and Wanted
Forsaken, Abandoned, Alone, and Forgotten	Knowing and Feeling Desirable Versus Undesirable (Chapter 7)	Confident, Prepared, Courageous, and Fearless
Restlessness, Unsettled, Ill-at-ease, and Anxiousness	Knowing and Feeling Capable Versus Powerless (Chapter 6)	Purified, Forgiven, Cleansed, and Acquitted

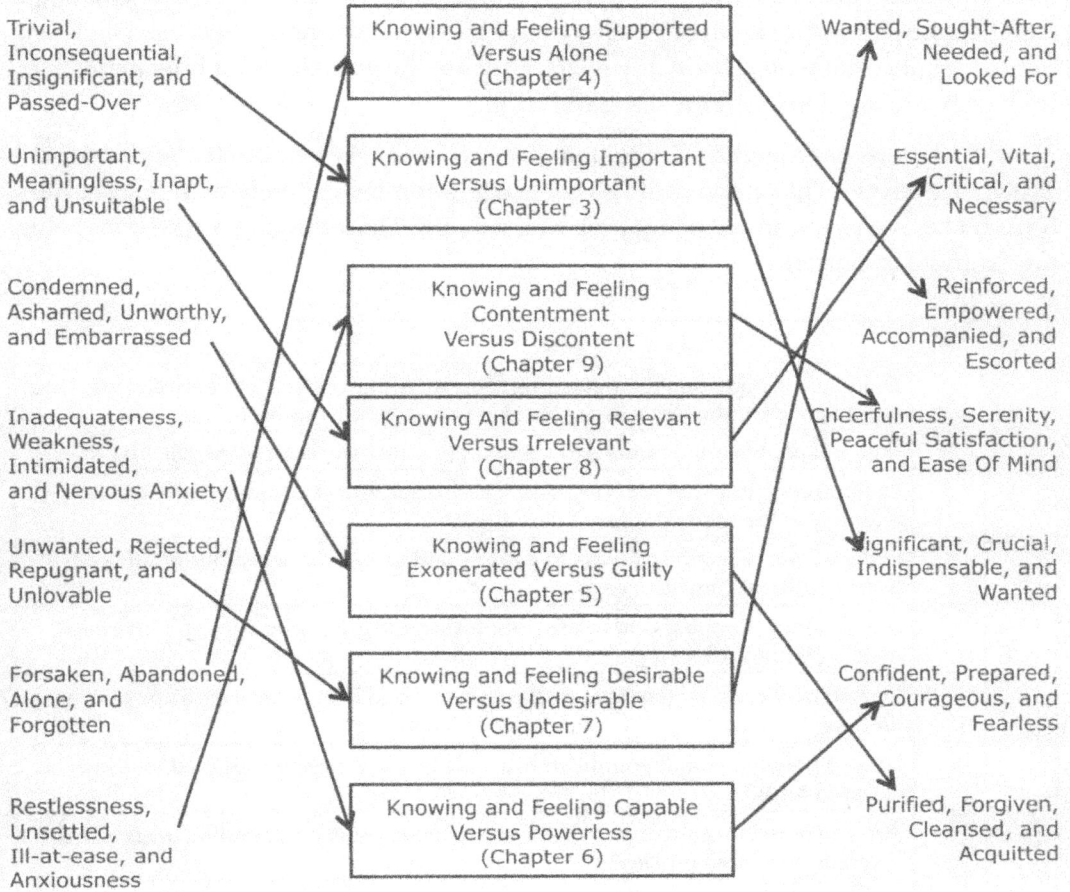

WHERE ARE YOU NOW?

How to determine if this book has set you on a path to a freeing relationship with Christ

This book starts you on a journey … it is not an end unto itself.

So how did you do on the exercise on the previous page? I'm concerned that you might feel that you did not do well, or you may have given up altogether because you found it too difficult. That would break my heart. Here are the guidelines for how to interpret how well you are doing after reading the book.

Note: Each of us has a slightly different interpretation of each emotion identified in the previous exercise. That alone could easily account for any differences in our answers. So don't be overly concerned about how well you did. The following conclusions below are far more important.

YES	NO	
		Did you conclude that there is a direct and important correlation between how you feel and each of the seven love gaps that may exist in your life?
		Will you allow your emotions to alert you to the existence of a possible love gap?
		Did you conclude that Jesus can and will fill each and every love gap associated with any of the seven desires of your heart?
		Did you find new biblical ways to address and satisfy the seven desires of your heart to mitigate any love gaps?
		Are you now allowing God to use your feelings to guide you back to a love gap needing your attention?
		Do you now see how that Jesus is the only real and lasting answer to any and every love gap?
		Do you now know that your heart has built-in seven desires designed to draw you closer to Jesus?
		Are you now more attentive as to how you are currently responding to each of the seven desires of your heart?
		Do you now understand that all your friends are battling their individual seven desires of their hearts, and this book has given you ways to help them fill their personal love gaps?
		Do you now have a greater appreciation of God's design of your heart and how He has created you in such a way that you are constantly and consistently being drawn to Him and allowing Him to love you in a way that only He can do?
		Do you now know that you never, ever are a victim, and that God uses everything to put you in a better position to receive His love and get you ready for a forever relationship with Him?

Leader's Resource Guide

For Small Group Bible Study Leaders

Then I heard the voice of the Lord saying,

"Whom shall I send?

And who will go for us?"

And I said,

"Here am I. Send me!"

Isaiah 6:8, NIV

Preparing to Lead

PARTNERING WITH GOD TO MAKE A DIFFERENCE

Would you like to know how you got here? **(You may think you know, but you don't!)**

I'm so glad you are reading this, and I thank you for making yourself available to God to be an answer to our prayers for leaders of this critical study. He has selected you and nudged you to accept His calling. Here is the prayer that God answered through your willing and open heart.

Allow me to share with you just how that happened and what was going on behind the scenes. I think you will find it very interesting and validating. Because we are very limited as to the number of people we all know, we had to ask God to do what He had requested Moses to do in Numbers 27:18. *So the LORD said to Moses, "Take Joshua son of Nun, a man in whom is the spirit of leadership, and lay your hand on him"* (NIV). (Emphasis mine) In short, God selected and brought you here as a direct answer to our prayers for leaders. He is the one who tapped you on the shoulder. Thank you again for saying yes and making yourself accessible to God. You have the *spirit of leadership* identified in that Scripture, or you wouldn't be reading this right now. Regardless of how you may personally feel, any doubts you may have, God has tapped you.

There are few, if any, studies that target the core aspirations in people's hearts like this approach does. It just doesn't get any more personal than these topics, and each topic contains the seeds of the future of a human being. And the seeds that they choose to water and feed will determine the kind of person they will ultimately become. And into that seed planting and watering process, you have now stepped. Your prayerful guidance of these readers makes you a partner with Christ in the most noble work on planet earth — the growing of a Christ-follower! You are playing a privileged role in people's emotional jailbreaks. You will be there every step on their journey to their increasing emotional freedom. You are playing a crucial role in moving them toward being set free from some of the most debilitating and defeating emotions with which Satan has kept them bound and daily crushes their spirit. May God richly bless you in your leadership. Here are five encouragements for you to remember along the way. Reproduce these and put them where you will see them throughout your day. Perhaps even commit to memorizing these Scriptures. Make this wisdom a part of your heart.

1. Be invigorated to give it all you've got! Ecclesiastes 9:10, NIV: *Whatever your hand finds to do, do it with all your might, for in the grave, where you are going, there is neither working nor planning nor knowledge nor wisdom.* (Emphasis mine) Don't let this opportunity to be a positive influence on people's lives pass you by. This is your time to yield precious fruit; optimize it to the fullest! You and they will be forever

glad you did. Our time on earth is short. At some point, we will no longer have the opportunity to serve. Now is your time.

2. Don't get disheartened with some of your people's progress or the lack thereof. Being a leader isn't always easy, but don't give up. 2 Chronicles 15:7, NIV: *"But as for you, be strong and <u>do not give up</u>, for <u>your work will be rewarded."</u>* (Emphasis mine) The day will come in heaven when these people participating in your study will be the greatest source of your heavenly joy! Lean into any discomfort, as the work of planting a seed is work and can be challenging.

3. You will never be alone as you lead this study. A good leader is always listening to and for God's directions. Isaiah 30:21, NIV: *Whether you turn to the right or to the left, <u>your ears will hear a voice behind you</u>, saying, "This is the way; walk in it."* (Emphasis mine) God is so thrilled to be partnering with you. I promise you that when the study is done, you will look back at these days as one of the highlights of your stay on planet earth when you and God worked hand in hand to set people free to be what God designed them to become!

4. There is always help for you as the leader when, at times, you feel inadequate. James 1:5, NIV: *<u>If any of you lacks wisdom, he should ask God</u> who gives generously to all without finding fault, and it will be given to him.* (Emphasis mine) There are three reasons why He is eager to hear and answer your prayers: a) He loves you, b) He loves what you are doing, and c) He loves whom you are doing it with!

5. Remember that your role is NOT to harvest, but to plant. A good leader must exercise patience. Proverbs 16:32, NIV. *<u>Better a patient man than a warrior</u>, a man who controls his temper than one who takes a city.* (Emphasis mine) There are great victories in the futures of your participants that you will never witness until heaven. For now, just plant, water and believe!

Know that the Holy Spirit is in your meetings and showing up in different ways. Know that a miracle is happening. Also, know that this may mean that the unpredictable may need room in your carefully planned meeting or calendar. Give yourself permission to **not** complete an agenda in one meeting, as you may need a continuance to the next meeting. This experience may not fit neatly into our perfectly planned marching orders of agendas over 12 weeks. Set this expectation with your group.

Know that vulnerability and self-disclosure starts with you. Your authenticity and courage to share will open the doors for others. Prepare stories to share for each meeting when needed. Read the activities and do your own work beforehand. Here is a quote from Brené Brown to lean on: "Vulnerability sounds like truth and feels like courage. Truth and courage aren't always comfortable, but they're never weakness." (From *Daring Greatly: How the Courage to Be Vulnerable Transforms the Way We Live, Love, Parent, and Lead*)

Thank you again! I wish you Godspeed and I already know that God will richly bless you and your leadership, both now and in eternity!

LaVon

Why the Bible Study you are leading is the very best way to develop people for Christ

(This is what theologians call sanctification.)

Many people are not aware of the dangers of being overexposed to too much truth in too little time. But there are real hazards to be avoided. I know it may sound strange, but here are some caution areas where you could be at risk when reading a book like *Untangling the Seven Desires of Your Heart* alone or in some airplane seat. Here are the principles upon which your small group study is built and why it can be so very successful in transforming lives.

- **Caution #1: Becoming educated beyond your level of obedience.** Often we go to church and hear good truth that is piled onto the truth we heard last week, which was piled on top of the truth heard the week before, etc. And each time we hear new truth, we can often forget about, and stop trying to obey, the truth we had heard the week before.

  As the gap between what we are doing (obeying) and what we are knowing (learning) widens, we can get a form of spiritual schizophrenia where we will find ourselves reading and feeling emotionless about the wonderful, life-changing new truths. This is because we are emotionally exhausted and feeling guilty from knowing so much more than we are currently doing, and we become emotionally numb to acquiring even more new truths. We cannot allow ourselves to get excited about more new truth that we know will likely not be integrated into our daily lives. Don't let this book or any book educate you beyond your level of obedience. We have a choice that must be made: either slow down the intake of new truth so we can assimilate it into our lives or speed up the process of allocating a Holy Spirit led, deliberate response as to what we are learning and what should become our obedience focus.

  In some ways, the first members of the emerging Church in the first century had a very different experience than do we today. When they met, they didn't yet have a Bible, or a recorder, or radio/TV so it was a bunch of people sharing what they heard Peter or Paul saying, and they talked about these brand-new truths in an excited and embracing way. Each person would share what they heard and what they felt it meant. And they often met on a daily basis for these types of hear and say discussions in their homes.

  They broke bread in their homes and ate together with glad and sincere hearts, praising God and enjoying the favor of all the people" Acts 2:46b-47a (NIV).

Contrast that to us today. When I'm not traveling, I may hear two sermons a day on the car radio just driving to and from our corporate office. In today's wired world, we live with an abundance of opportunities for hearing new truth, so this problem is greater for us today than for the first-century Christians. With so much truth instantly available, it forces us to have to make more Holy Spirit guided decisions as to which truth He wants us to focus on at that time. While it is a blessing to have so much truth available to us, it comes with a responsibility to become more prayerfully discerning with a willing response.

The Bible study you are leading enables your participants to go at a learning pace that is conducive to transformative application. They will be engaged in multiple conversations concerning multiple implementation approaches in their lives. They can confront each other, motivate each other, challenge each other, and pray for each other. And they can do all of this with one truth at a time! That is why your small group study can be so effective and used by God in a big way!

- **Caution #2: Truth heard once and not acted upon can be worse than truth never heard at all**. In much the same manner that a flu shot or a smallpox vaccination works, where your body will build up an immunity system against the flu or smallpox in the future, the same can happen when hearing truth and not embracing it, obeying it, or believing in it; it can actually immune you to ever really hearing it and acting on it in the future. When you hear it again, it's old news and you say, "I've heard that before" and dismiss it. Satan is hoping you will be overwhelmed by all that you are hearing and is counting on your inaction and future dismissal. By not acting on new truths, you may have ruined it for your future. The truth and its power may have been lost to you, perhaps even forever.

  That is why you are cautioned to be sensitive to the speed at which you are traveling on this journey to emotional freedom. This study was designed to take 12 weeks, but please be free to follow the pace of your participants. I know we live in a hurry-up world, but your participants deserve and need plenty of love time, prayer time, Holy Spirit conviction time, self-reflection time, and truth-processing time. Monitor the pace at which God is working in and through your group. When there is an ah-ha moment when and where truth collides with life, hit the pause button and trigger a transparent discussion so your participants have a chance to own the new truth and accept a responsibility to introduce it into the way they live.

- **A Biblical Directive** In Luke 11:28 Jesus replied, *"Blessed rather are those who hear the word of God and obey it"* (NIV). If the two academic principles above were confusing, this biblical directive is very simple and clear. The goal is not to finish the book but to grow in our likeness of Jesus. Hear and obey is that one-two punch that will make your Bible study transformative in nature.

So, given these two cautions plus the biblical directive, here are some of my heartfelt suggestions for you to consider as you begin your Bible Study group:

Please:

- Don't allow your participants to just read the book to check a box indicating that they've completed it and then go on to the next book on their list. Encourage them to make it their goal to be greater than just finishing another book. It is like going to church, you want them to come out of church closer to Christ than when they went in. Consider letting that be your prayer when leading this study. You want every participant to come out of the study more emotionally free than when they began.

- Don't be in a hurry when you are leading the study, allow God to stop you for essential periods of reflection and discussion. If you are not regularly hitting the pause button, you are probably rushing the study way too fast. I've provided you with more activities than you can complete in a session. Select the ones that are the most suitable for your group and prioritize them accordingly.

Please:

- When a new love-gap concept comes up and is revealed as a problem area, pause to discuss and pray it into your participant's lives. Some of these truths may be very hard truths for them to hear. Don't let them run or hide from them. Give God a chance to love the concept into their lives.

- Do ask the people reading the book with you hard questions in love as to how they are planning on applying these new breakthrough concepts into their lives. Invite them to ask you difficult questions in return. Let the verse in Proverbs 27:17 become a reality where it says, *As iron sharpens iron, so one person sharpens another* (NIV). (Emphasis mine) Let the sparks fly. If done in love, that is how growth happens.

- Do pray that your participants will understand God's love in a new and meaningful way each step of the way on their journey. Chances are they may have never read a book that had so much love in it. (The Bible, of course, being the greatest exception of all time.)

Remember, this book was written to advance the apostle Paul's directive in 2 Thessalonians 3:5 (NIV), where it says, *May the Lord direct your hearts into God's love and Christ's perseverance.* By both design and intent, every chapter in this book was deliberately written to overwhelm your participant's hearts with His fresh, inspiring love. You and they will discover new ways, new reasons and new places to experience God's love. Enjoy the journey and be ready to be amazed to find out just how much love you and they have been missing out on.

www.ingramcontent.com/pod-product-compliance
Lightning Source LLC
Chambersburg PA
CBHW081156090426
42736CB00017B/3346